HERE I AM! series

LOTTIE MOON

The Girl Who Reached the World

圣经

HOLY BIBLE

narrated by Mei Mei the Panda

Amy Whitfield

illustrated by Marcin Piwowarski

B&H kids

Brentwood TN

Dedicated to the millions of women fulfilling the Great Commission.

On page 21, you will see a letter Lottie wrote. Can you find the fourteen words from the letter hidden on the pages in this book?

Once upon a time, a little girl grew up in the countryside of Virginia with her family and her pets. Her name was Charlotte Digges Moon, but no one called her that. They all called her Lottie.

Hello from China!

I'm Mei Mei the panda. I have a story to tell you, but it begins on the other side of the world from me.

VIEWMONT, LOTTIE'S HOME

The

Lottie lived in a large house with a large family, and she had a busy life. There were always animals around, and the children loved to play and have fun.

Lottie had four sisters and two brothers. Of all seven, she was the feisty one who was most likely to misbehave.

Many girls did not attend school in those days, but Lottie was different. When she was fourteen, her family sent her to live and study at a school with other girls. The students were taught how to play musical instruments and speak other languages. She studied Latin and French (and later added Greek, Italian, and Spanish).

needs

Lottie was one of the smartest students in her class, but she had no interest in religion. She once played a prank on the other students by using towels to silence the bell that was supposed to wake them for chapel.

WOOF! WOOF!

When Lottie was a girl, her mother had told the children about God, but Lottie did not believe the stories about Jesus were real.

One night after she had just turned eighteen, Lottie was trying to sleep, but a barking dog was keeping her awake. As she lay in her bed, her mind raced, and she began to **think about God.**

Lottie finally decided that she should learn more about Him, so she visited a church. There she heard the story of Jesus and believed it! She was baptized right away.

By this time, Lottie was one of the first women in the South to earn a Master of Arts degree. She had become a teacher and hoped to one day travel the world.

But when she became a Christian, Lottie's dreams of traveling changed. Now she wanted to go and tell people about the good news of the gospel. She wanted her job to be reaching the world for Jesus.

When she was thirty-three, Lottie got her own good news—she and her sister were going to China! They were some of the first single women from America to be missionaries and tell people about Jesus.

People

AMERICA

Now, China is **a loooooong way** from Virginia. Lottie had to take a train all the way across the United States. And then she had to sail on a steamer ship all the way across the ocean.

CHINA

Have you ever been bored or tired on a long trip? Well, Lottie's trip to China took more than six weeks!

Lottie was finally in the countryside again, but this time it was on the other side of the world from Virginia. The countryside of China became her **new home.**

When Lottie traveled into villages, she sometimes rode in a sedan chair! People have been traveling this way in China for thousands of years.

She started teaching children just like she had in America, but then she began traveling and telling people about Jesus. The Chinese loved to see her, and she would sit under the trees to share the good news with anyone who would listen.

Lottie baked cookies for the children in the villages so often that they began to call her **the Cookie Lady!** They would come to her house for cookies but would learn from the Bible while they were there.

Lottie also talked to women in the villages, knowing they would listen to another woman. They were hearing the stories of Jesus for the first time!

Lottie loved her new friends so much and did whatever she could to connect with them. She changed how she dressed and wore her hair, and she lived in a house like the ones the people of China lived in. Instead of being someone who acted like she was from another place, she made **their home her home.**

LOTTIE'S HOUSE AT P'INGTU

Lottie didn't want to be different from her new friends. She was only 4 feet 3 inches tall, and that made it easy for the children to talk to her! She wore simple, loose clothes, just like them. She ate the same food and learned to use chopsticks like they did. Some days she ate eggs for every meal!

Lottie loved the people of China and knew more missionaries were needed to help them. She wrote hundreds of letters back to America to tell the stories of the Chinese—their lives, their needs, and how they needed to hear about Jesus.

The needs of this people press upon my soul and I cannot be silent.

Lottie hoped that if she talked about the people and the work, the people back home would care. Her stories were printed in newspapers that went to the churches. Even people who had never met her felt like they knew her and that she was a friend to everyone.

As a child, Lottie had been full of energy and not afraid to speak her mind. She now was able to use her words to talk to the people back home. She wrote hundreds of letters by hand since there were no computers or even a typewriter. She used the power of her pen to ask for help for the Chinese.

soul

Lottie and the other missionaries in China had so much to do and so many people to reach. But there wasn't enough money to bring more workers all the way across the ocean.

Lottie heard that groups of women back in America were creating clubs and working together to help people or to make changes in the world. So she had an idea. What if the women in American churches worked together to help the people of China?

The woman's club movement began as women gathered to discuss things they enjoyed. But then they started working together to make a difference. Some fought for women to be able to vote, while others focused on needs in their neighborhoods and in the nation.

Lottie grabbed her pen and began to write the churches, asking the women to collect money for China during a special time of year—Christmas! She thought that since people were already giving gifts to one another, they could give gifts for China too!

Everyone back home had heard of Lottie's wonderful work, so they were eager to help. The women started to work together to collect as many **nickels, dimes, quarters, and dollars** as they could. They called it a Christmas Offering.

This special offering didn't stop with China! The people raised money for missionaries **all around the world,** and year after year they continued. Finally, in 1918, the women decided to name the collection after Lottie so that everyone would remember how hard she worked and why they were giving.

THE LOTTIE MOON CHRISTMAS OFFERING:
Helping Missionaries Across the World

Today, people still give to the Lottie Moon Christmas Offering each year, and you can too!

Lottie stayed in China for the rest of
her life and was most concerned for
the people she had come to reach.
She continued to serve them until
her very last day. Although she was
lonely sometimes, she had friends
by her side who looked up to her and
wanted to be like Lottie.

When she became very sick, her friends took care of her. They wondered if taking her home to Virginia might help her get well, so they put her on a ship to America. Sadly, she was too sick and died on Christmas Eve while she was at sea. Lottie was seventy-two years old and had been a missionary for thirty-nine years, spending more than half her life doing what she loved!

Lottie wanted to show other women they had
important work to do and could make a difference.
She encouraged the leaders who sent her to China
to listen to the women and let them help.

Because of her tireless work, other girls were able to become missionaries and tell people near and far about **Jesus!**

Lottie's story has inspired women and girls for more than one hundred years. No matter their age or their work or their place in the world, they can bravely follow God's plan, just like Lottie.

Today, the people in China still remember Lottie Moon and her work. The church where she went each week now has about four thousand members, and the building is a protected historic site to preserve Lottie's story for years to come.

WULIN SHENGHUI CHURCH

基督教堂

Charlotte Digges Moon was much like any other girl. God woke her up to know Him, and she didn't rest until she told the world His story. Through the simple acts of baking cookies and writing letters—and quite a bit of feisty determination—Lottie's dream of **reaching the world for Jesus came true.**